# DOG
# Trainer

by Marie Pearson

CAPSTONE PRESS
a capstone imprint

Bright Idea Books are published by Capstone Press
1710 Roe Crest Drive, North Mankato, Minnesota 56003
www.mycapstone.com

**Library of Congress Cataloging-in-Publication Data**
Names: Pearson, Marie, author.
Title: Dog trainer / by Marie Pearson.
Description: North Mankato, Minnesota : Bright Idea Books, an imprint of
   Capstone Press, [2019] | Series: Jobs with animals | Audience: Age 9-12. |
   Audience: Grade 4 to 6. | Includes bibliographical references and index.
Identifiers: LCCN 2018035985 | ISBN 9781543557862 (hardcover : alk. paper) |
   ISBN 9781543558180 (ebook) | ISBN 9781543560480 (paperback)
Subjects: LCSH: Dog trainers--Vocational guidance--Juvenile literature.
Classification: LCC SF431 .P398 2019 | DDC 636.7/0887--dc23
LC record available at https://lccn.loc.gov/2018035985

**Editorial Credits**
Editor: Meg Gaertner
Designer: Becky Daum
Production Specialist: Dan Peluso

**Photo Credits**
iStockphoto: andresr, cover, 8–9, bloodstone, 12–13, cglade, 11, cunfek, 7, 28, FatCamera, 19, FotoimperiyA, 26, Jmichi, 20–21, mayalain, 6–7, wjenningsphotography, 14–15; Newscom: UPPA/Photoshot, 25; Shutterstock Images: Africa Studio, 20, Juha Saastamoinen, 23, Masarik, 5, otsphoto, 30–31, Rimma Mans, 16–17

Printed in the United States of America.
PA48

# TABLE OF CONTENTS

CHAPTER ONE
## DOG TRAINER.................. 4

CHAPTER TWO
## QUALITIES AND SKILLS ..... 10

CHAPTER THREE
## THE WORKPLACE ............. 18

CHAPTER FOUR
## EDUCATION..................... 22

Glossary ............................ 28
Other Jobs to Consider........ 29
Activity ............................. 30
Further Resources.............. 32
Index................................. 32

# CHAPTER 1

# DOG Trainer

Five people lead their puppies in a circle. A trainer watches them. She teaches the owners how to train their dogs. One puppy pulls on its leash. The owner keeps his puppy's attention with treats.

Another puppy ignores the treats. Its owner gives it a toy instead. The puppy loves the toy. The owners learned these tricks from the dog trainer.

It is good to train puppies before they learn bad behaviors.

In one agility event, dogs weave through poles quickly.

Some dog trainers train dogs for people. They might teach dogs how to hunt. They might train service dogs to **retrieve** dropped items.

Other trainers teach people how to train their own dogs. They help owners teach their dogs manners. They help owners prepare dogs for **agility** and other sports.

Dogs might jump over poles in agility events.

Giving treats is one way to reward dogs for good behavior.

Sometimes dogs learn unsafe behaviors. They might **lunge** at other dogs on walks. They might jump on a child. Trainers help owners teach dogs the right way to behave.

# TRICK AND TREAT

A dog performs a trick. It shakes hands, sits on command, or fetches. The trainer gives the dog a treat. This is repeated many times. The dog will eventually do the trick without the treat.

# CHAPTER 2

# QUALITIES and Skills

Dog trainers need to love animals. Some dogs may not want to work with people. Some might be **aggressive**. Trainers need to be patient. They should be positive. They find ways to help dogs want to behave.

Dog trainers develop good relationships with dogs.

Trainers must work well
with many different people.

# WORKING WITH PEOPLE

Trainers need to be good with people. They work with dog owners. Dogs do not always want to work with owners. Trainers show owners how to help dogs learn. They tell owners if they are doing something wrong. Trainers must do this kindly.

People with all kinds of dogs hire trainers. Trainers must be **confident** around all dogs. They should also know how to be safe with dogs. Dogs see certain body language as a threat. This includes bending over a dog. Trainers know which body language to use.

Dogs are often more comfortable when people kneel to greet them.

# BODY LANGUAGE

Dogs pay attention to people's eye contact and body position. They react differently to different tones of voice. Trainers know how to use this in training.

Trainers and owners must be careful not to give dogs too many treats. This can harm dogs' health.

# KNOWING THE DIFFERENCES

Dogs are all different. Some are active. Others are lazy. Some will work for food or toys. Others only want to be petted. Trainers learn how to get the best results from each dog. Knowing about different dog breeds is helpful. Most Labrador retrievers work for food. Punishments do not work well for greyhounds. Knowing these things helps trainers teach each dog.

# CHAPTER 3

# THE Workplace

Dog trainers can work anywhere there are dogs. Some own their own businesses. Some work for other trainers. Pet clinics and pet stores may hire trainers. Other trainers work at animal shelters. Some travel to people's homes.

Dog trainers often hold classes outside.

Police dogs work closely with specific officers.

Trainers may teach group classes. Some also do **private** lessons. Other trainers **board** several dogs. They train each dog for specific jobs.

These jobs might be hunting or protection. Guard dogs learn to protect certain people. They keep people safe from danger.

Hunting dogs might chase birds out of the grass for their owners.

**CHAPTER 4**

# EDUCATION

Trainers do not need to go to college. They should have experience training dogs. Many trainers teach dogs to compete in events such as **obedience**.

This shows clients that a trainer knows how to train dogs. Some trainers teach classes on dog sports. These trainers should have experience competing in that sport.

Dogs that compete in agility may learn to jump through agility rings.

Some trainers are famous. Cesar Millan and Victoria Stilwell have had their own TV shows. Canadian Susan Garrett is a star trainer in agility.

There are many dog-training **methods**. Trainers need to know how dogs learn. Reading about training is important. Some experts hold workshops. They teach other trainers about specific topics. This might include how to train aggressive dogs. People can also take classes online.

Victoria Stilwell has written many books about dog training.

25

Trainers make sure pets are well behaved.

People who want to be trainers can learn from trainers. They can help with classes. They watch the trainers work.

Dog training does not pay very well. Trainers make between $21,000 and $34,000 per year. But dog training is a rewarding job. Trainers help dogs and people work together. They make having dogs safe and fun.

# GLOSSARY

**aggressive**
mean or hostile

**agility**
a dog sport in which dogs go
through an obstacle course
and are scored on speed
and accuracy

**board**
to house and feed

**confident**
assured and not afraid
or nervous

**lunge**
to move forward suddenly
and forcefully

**method**
a way of doing something

**obedience**
a dog event in which dogs are
scored on how well they obey
their handlers in certain tasks

**private**
not involving anyone else

**retrieve**
to get and bring back

# OTHER JOBS TO CONSIDER

## DOG WALKER

Dog walkers walk dogs when owners are unable to do so. Dog walkers may walk many dogs at once. They need to be good trainers too. They teach dogs not to pull on the leash.

## PET GROOMER

Pet groomers keep pets clean. They most often work with dogs and cats. They trim nails, give baths, and brush fur. They also give pets haircuts.

## VETERINARIAN

Veterinarians keep pets healthy. Some vets work with cats, dogs, and other small pets. Other vets work with larger animals such as horses and cows. Veterinarians examine pets to make sure they are healthy. If a pet is sick, they treat the animal so it gets better.

# ACTIVITY

## DOG WATCHING

Many cities have dog parks. These are fenced areas of land. People bring their dogs to the park. The dogs can run around safely. They can also play with other dogs.

Find a dog park near you. Watch the dogs and their owners. Do the dogs listen to their owners? How do the owners get their dogs to behave? Do they use toys or treats?

# FURTHER RESOURCES

**Interested in being a dog trainer? Learn more here:**

American Kennel Club: How to Become a Dog Trainer
www.akc.org/expert-advice/training/basic-training/want-to-be-dog-trainer/

Animal Humane Society: Becoming a Dog Trainer
www.animalhumanesociety.org/becoming-dog-trainer

Sundance, Kyra. *101 Dog Tricks, Kids Edition: Fun and Easy Activities, Games, and Crafts*. Beverly, Mass.: Quarry Books, 2014.

**Curious about different types of dog training?
Check out these websites:**

PBS Learning Media: Agility
https://tpt.pbslearningmedia.org/resource/8a4d516a-19b6-4eed-ab30-12c41b728029/8a4d516a-19b6-4eed-ab30-12c41b728029/

PBS Learning Media: Search-and-Rescue Dogs
https://tpt.pbslearningmedia.org/resource/45c5d92b-10da-4e76-88db-185c2e82f45c/45c5d92b-10da-4e76-88db-185c2e82f45c/

# INDEX

agility, 7, 24

body language, 14, 15

classes, 20, 23–24, 27

dog breeds, 17
dog owners, 4–5, 7–8, 13

Garrett, Susan, 24
guard dogs, 21

hunting, 21

leashes, 4

Millan, Cesar, 24

obedience, 22

service dogs, 6
Stilwell, Victoria, 24

toys, 5, 17
treats, 4–5, 9
tricks, 5, 9